AF379300

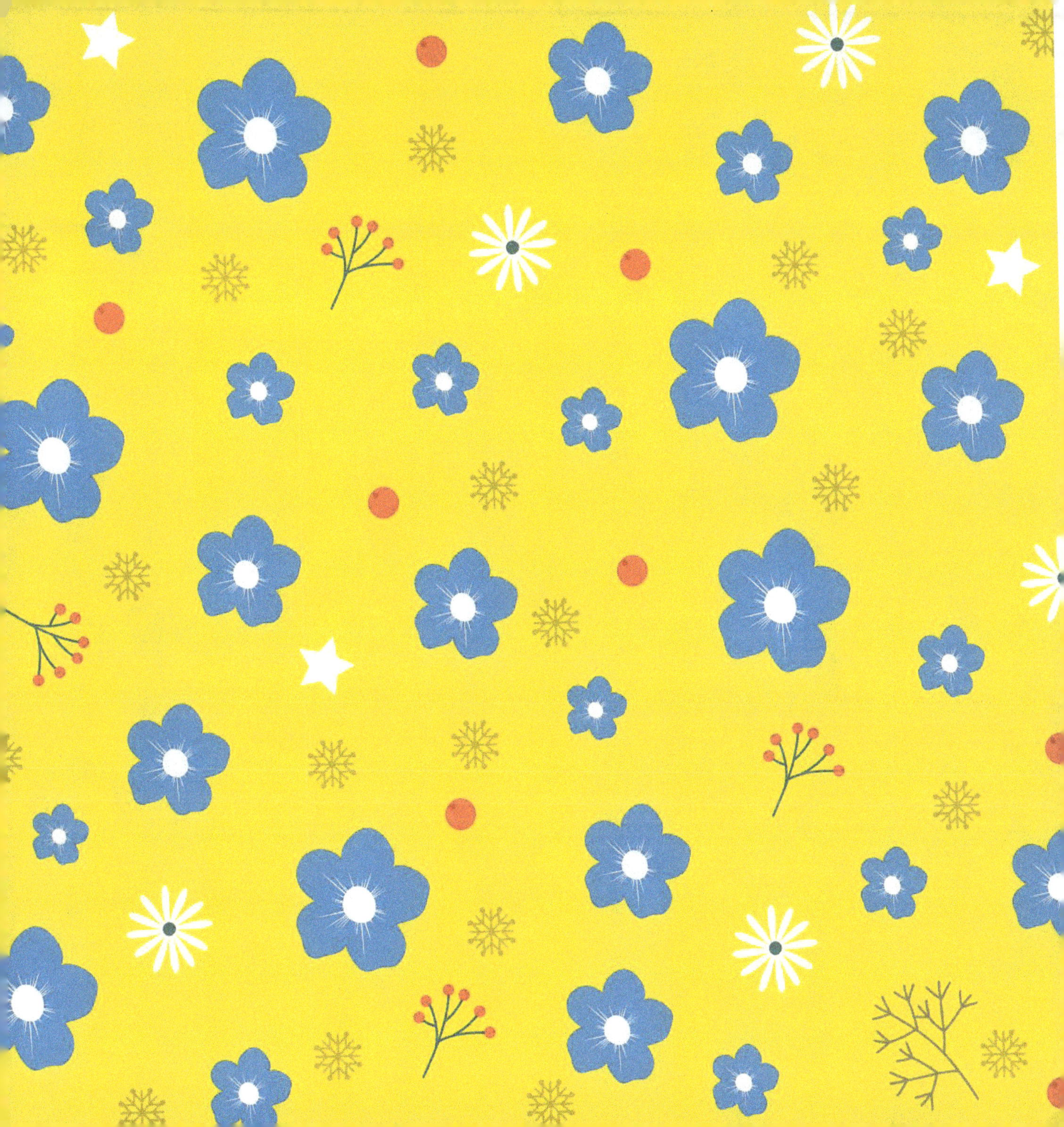

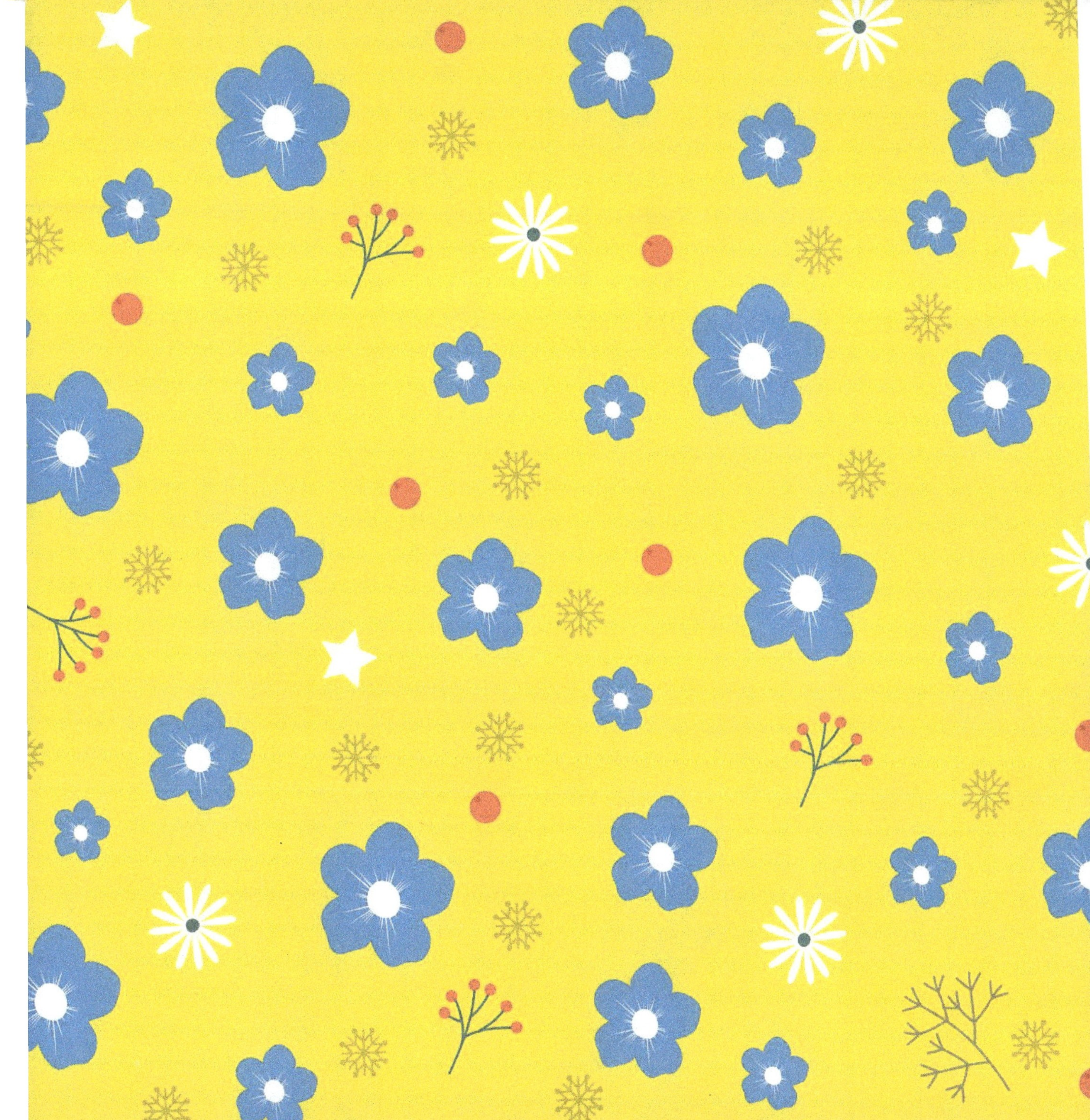

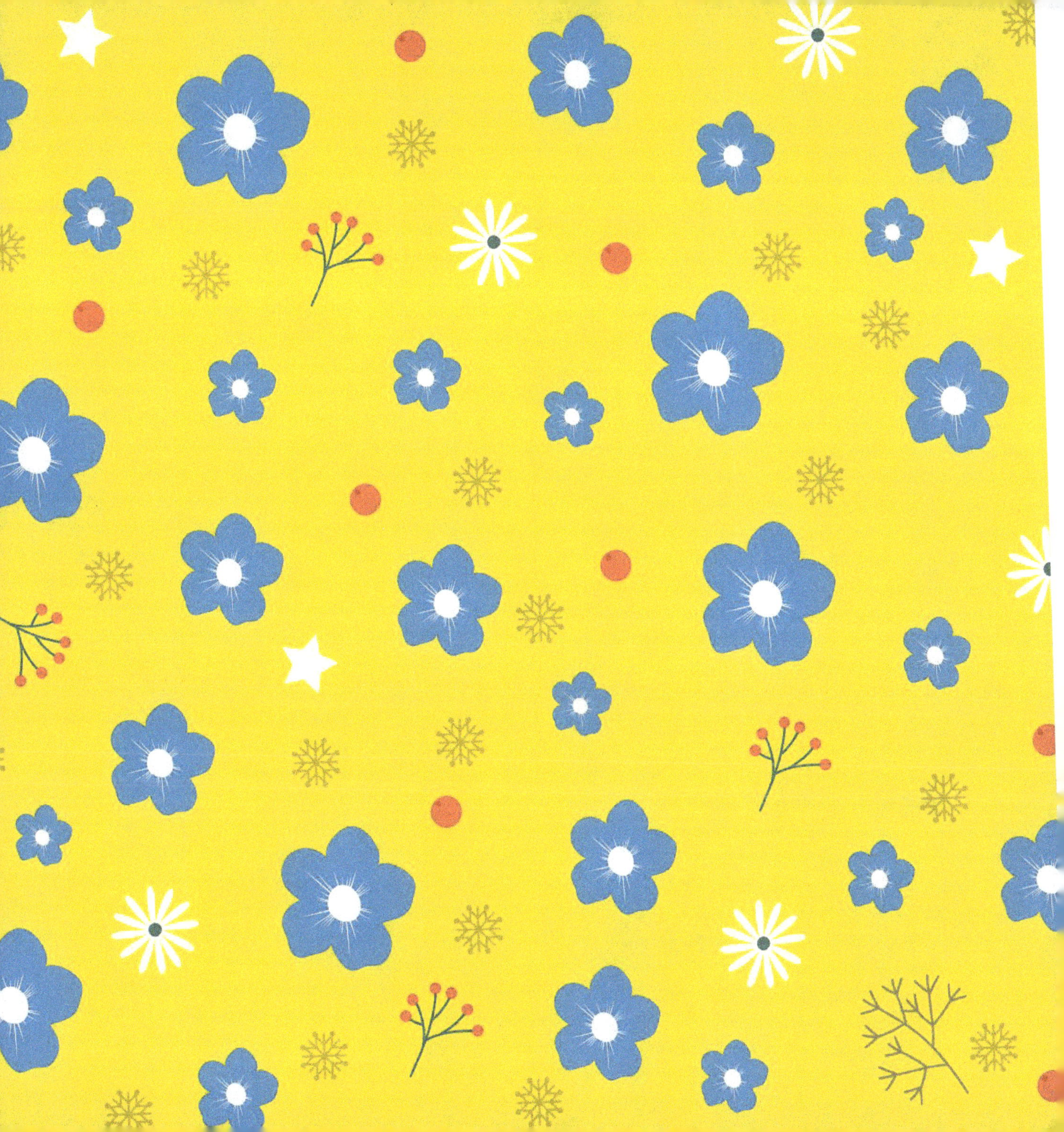

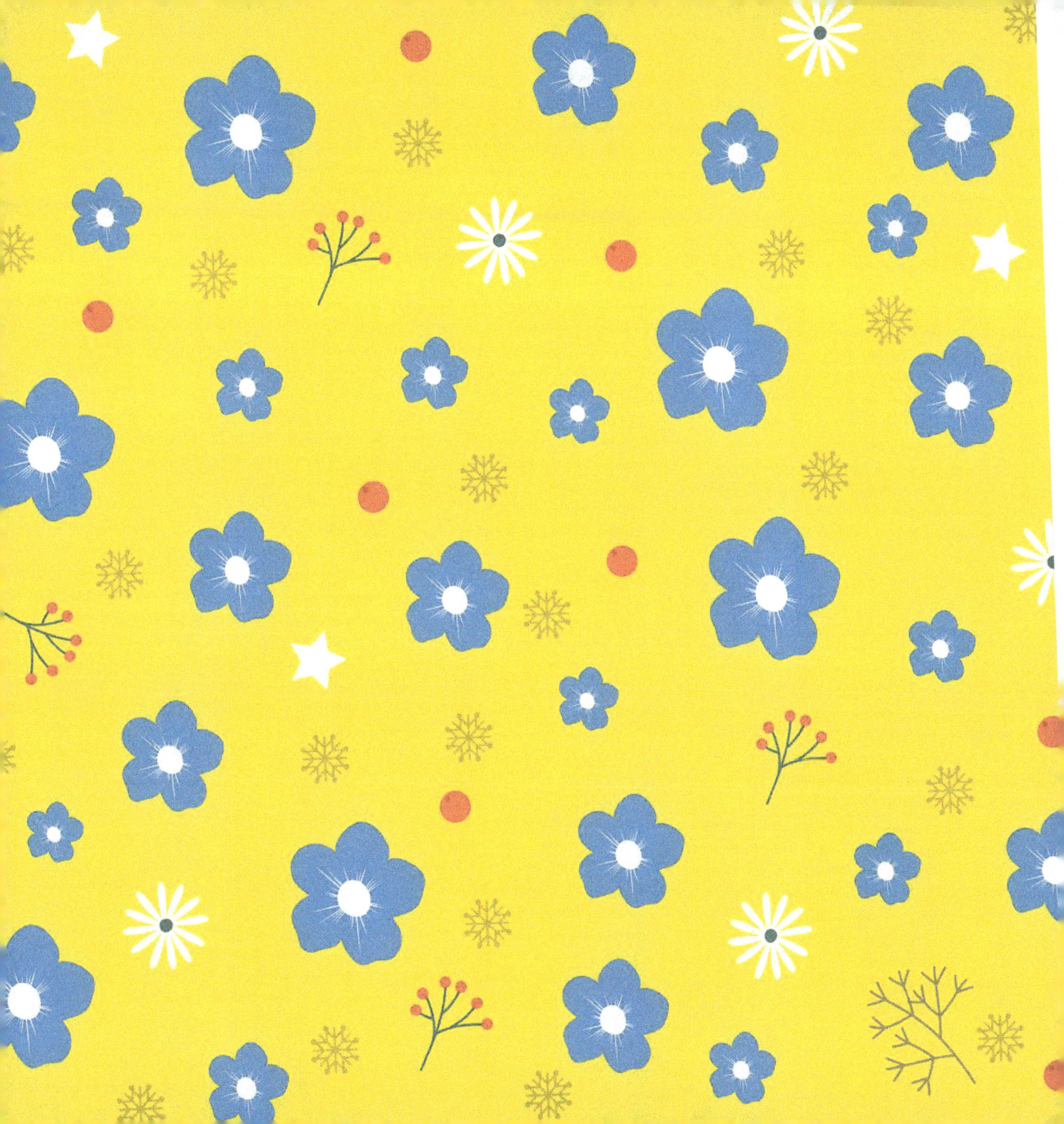

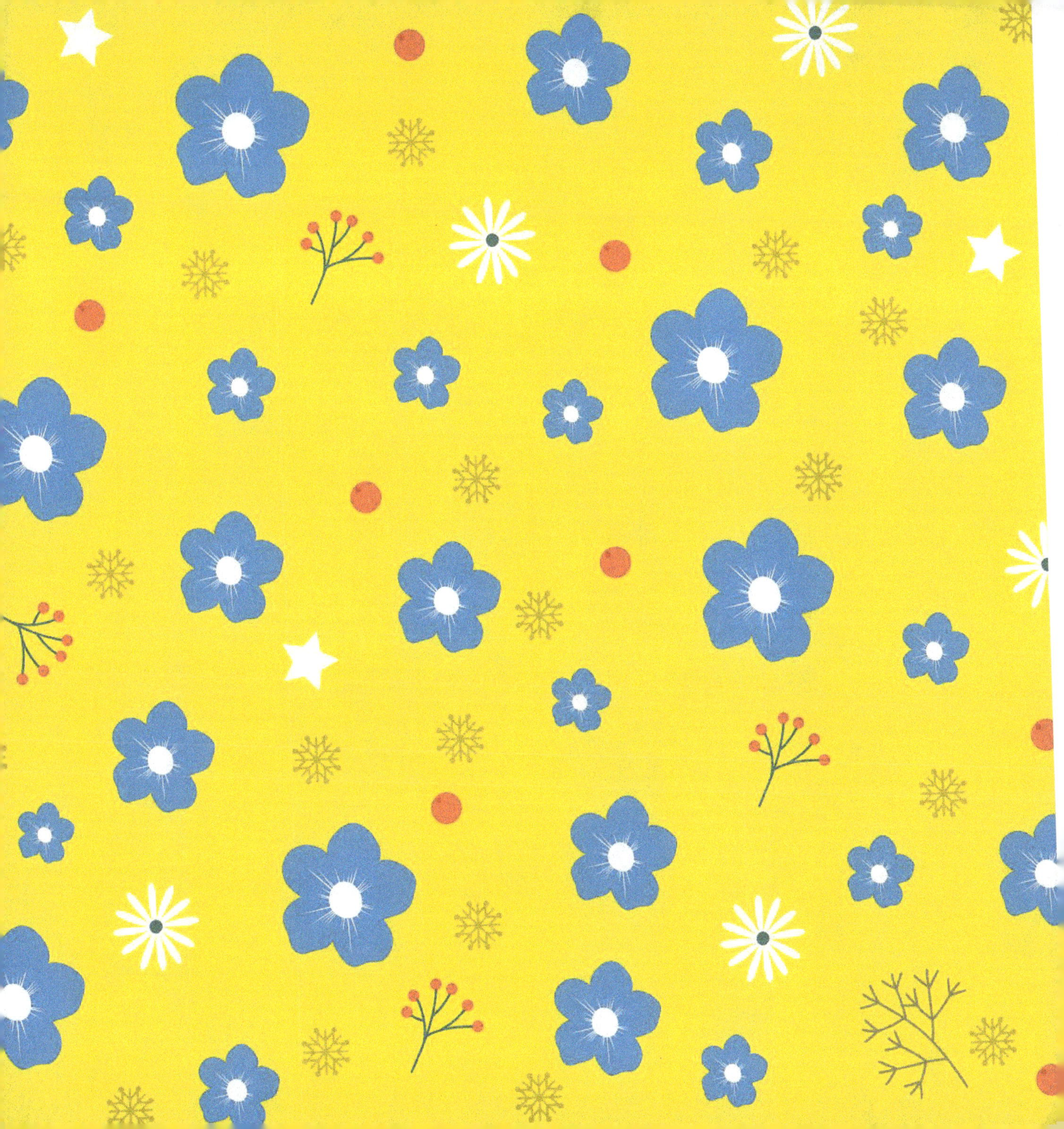

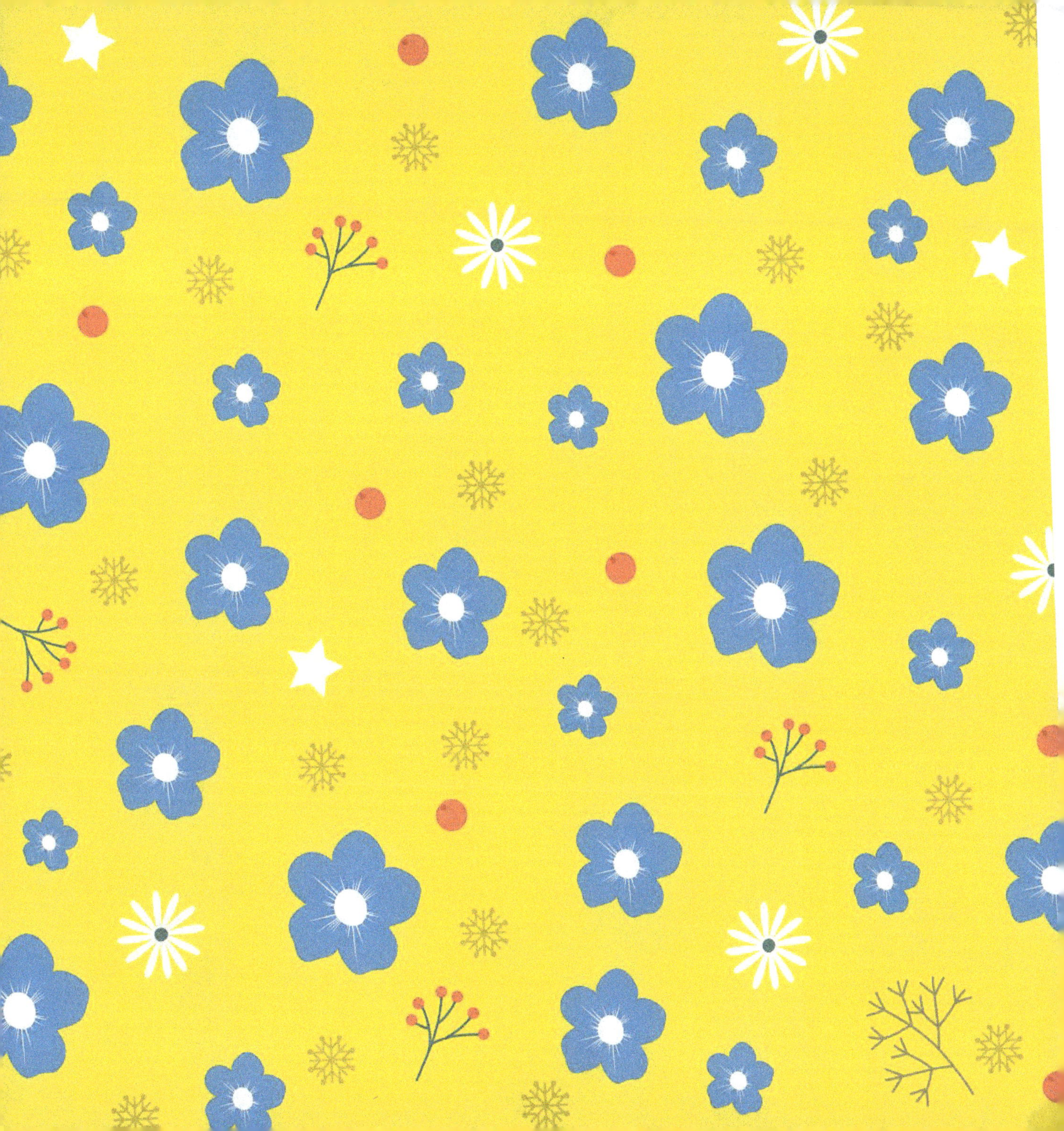

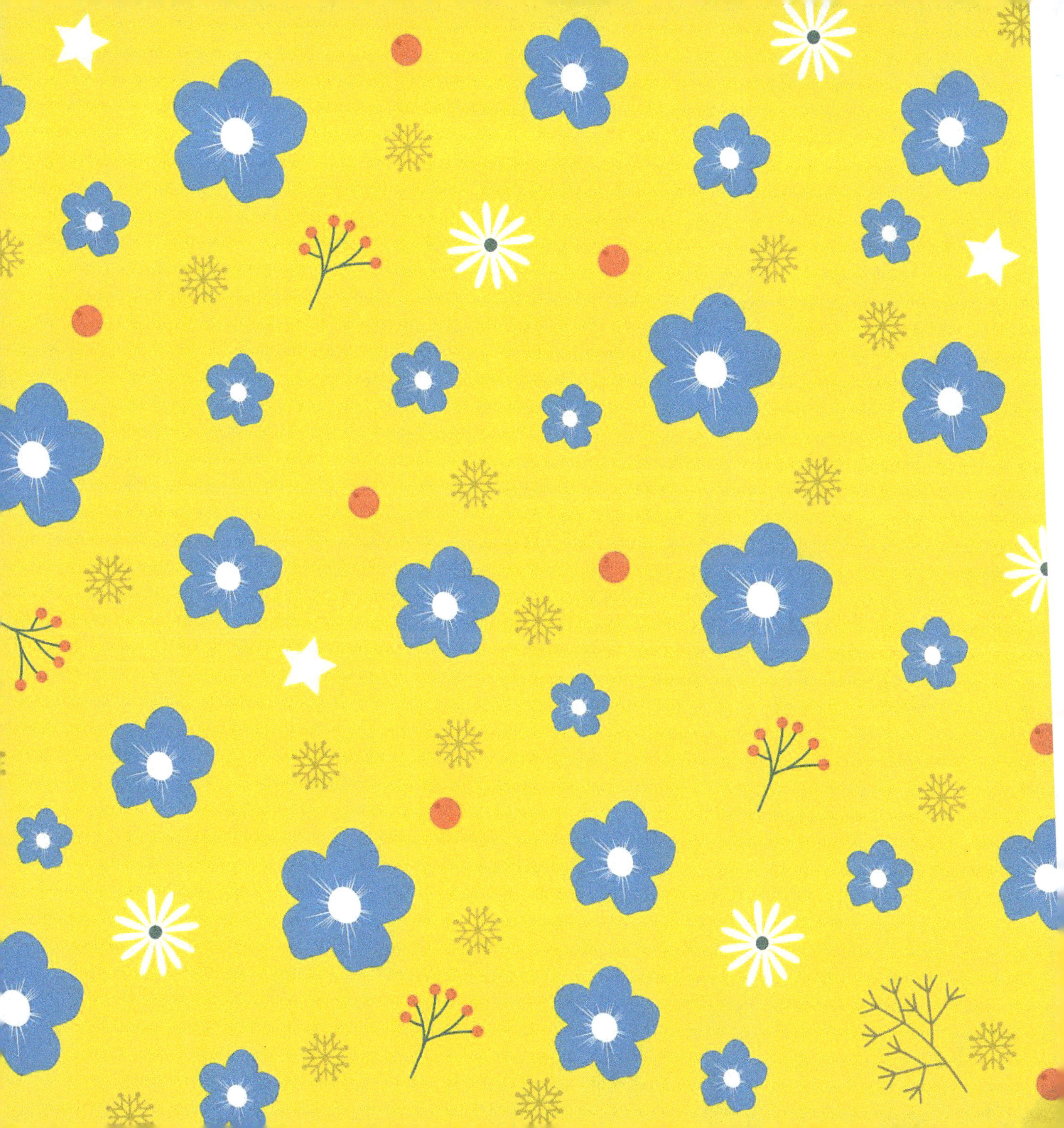

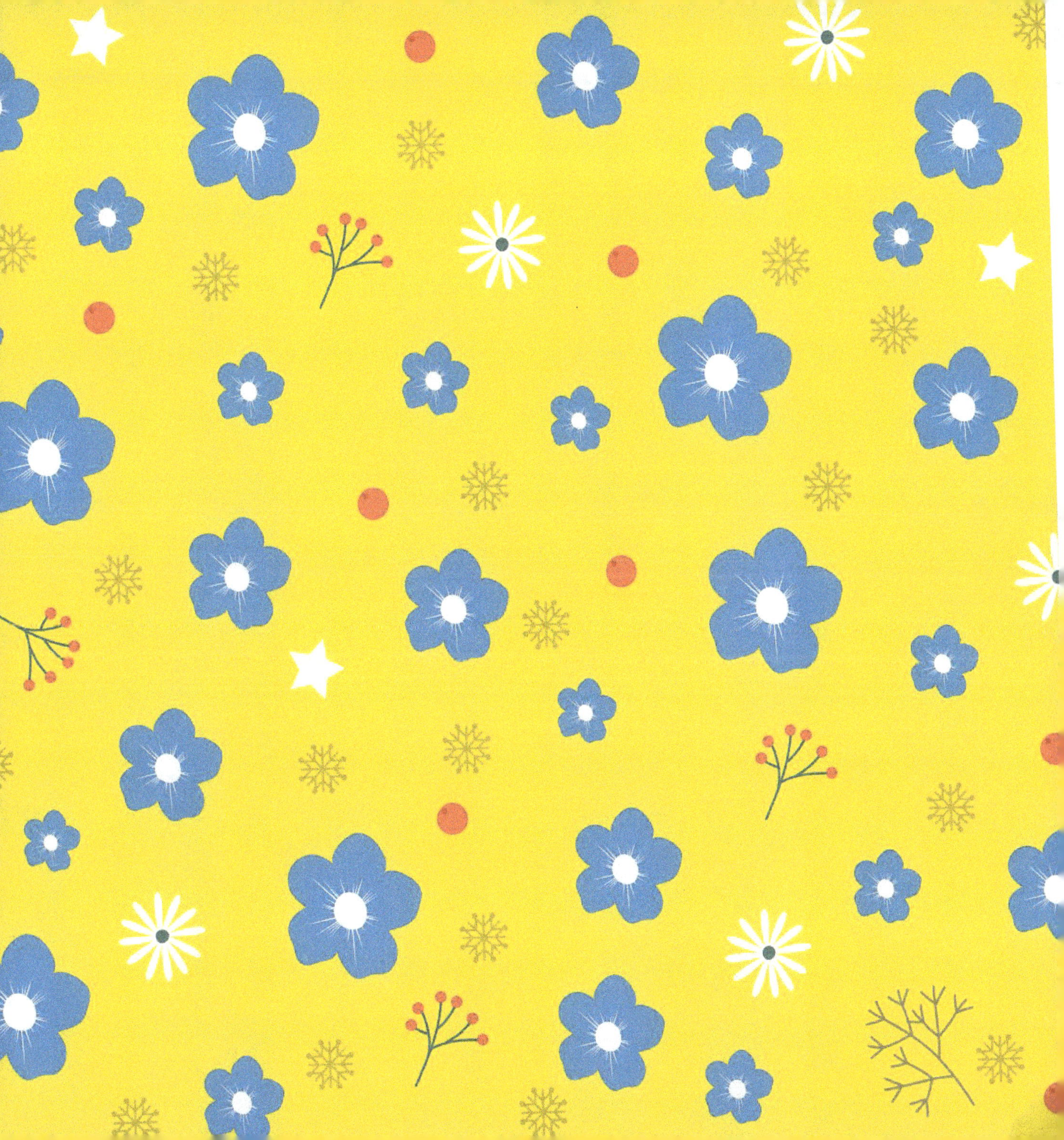

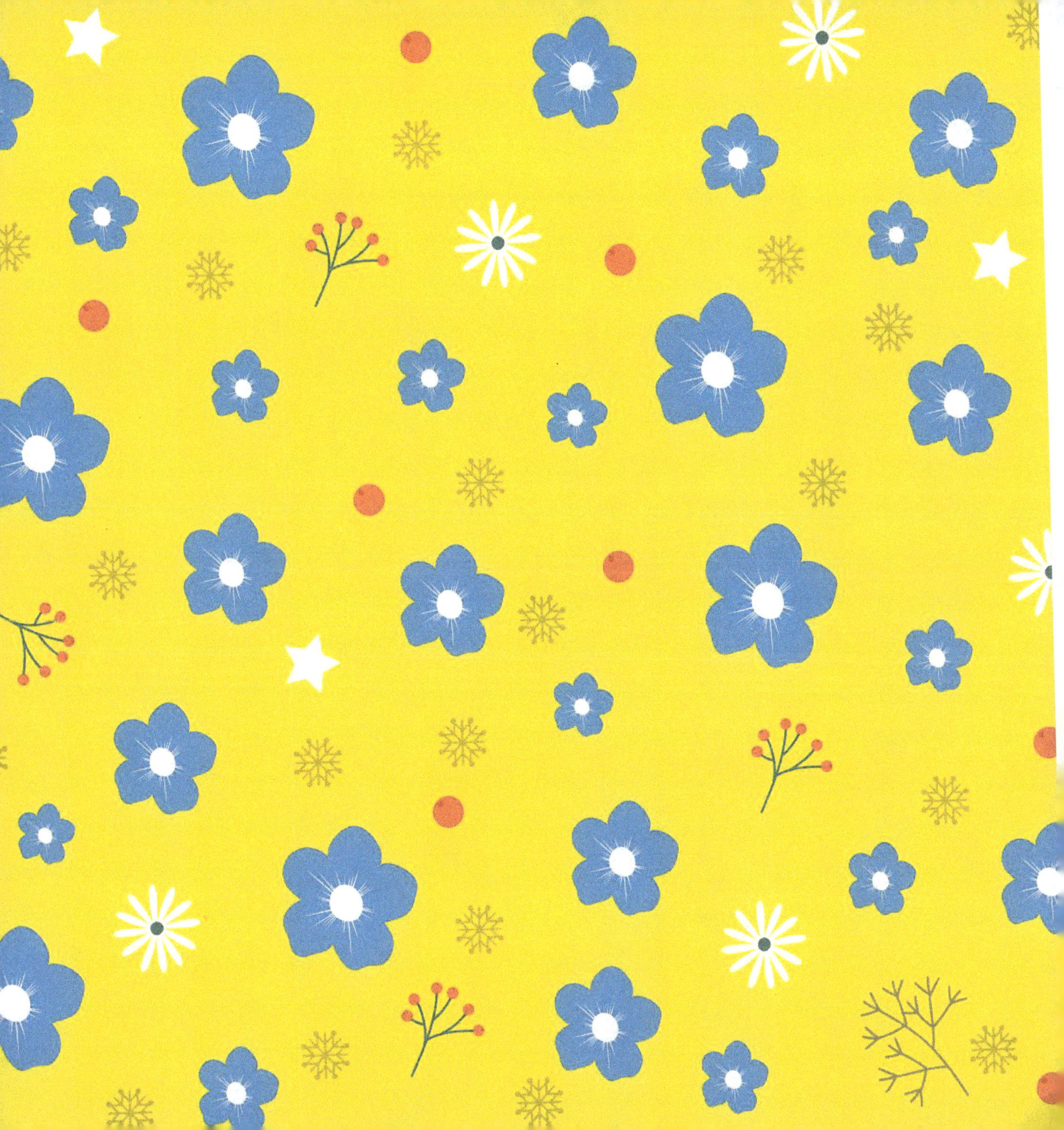

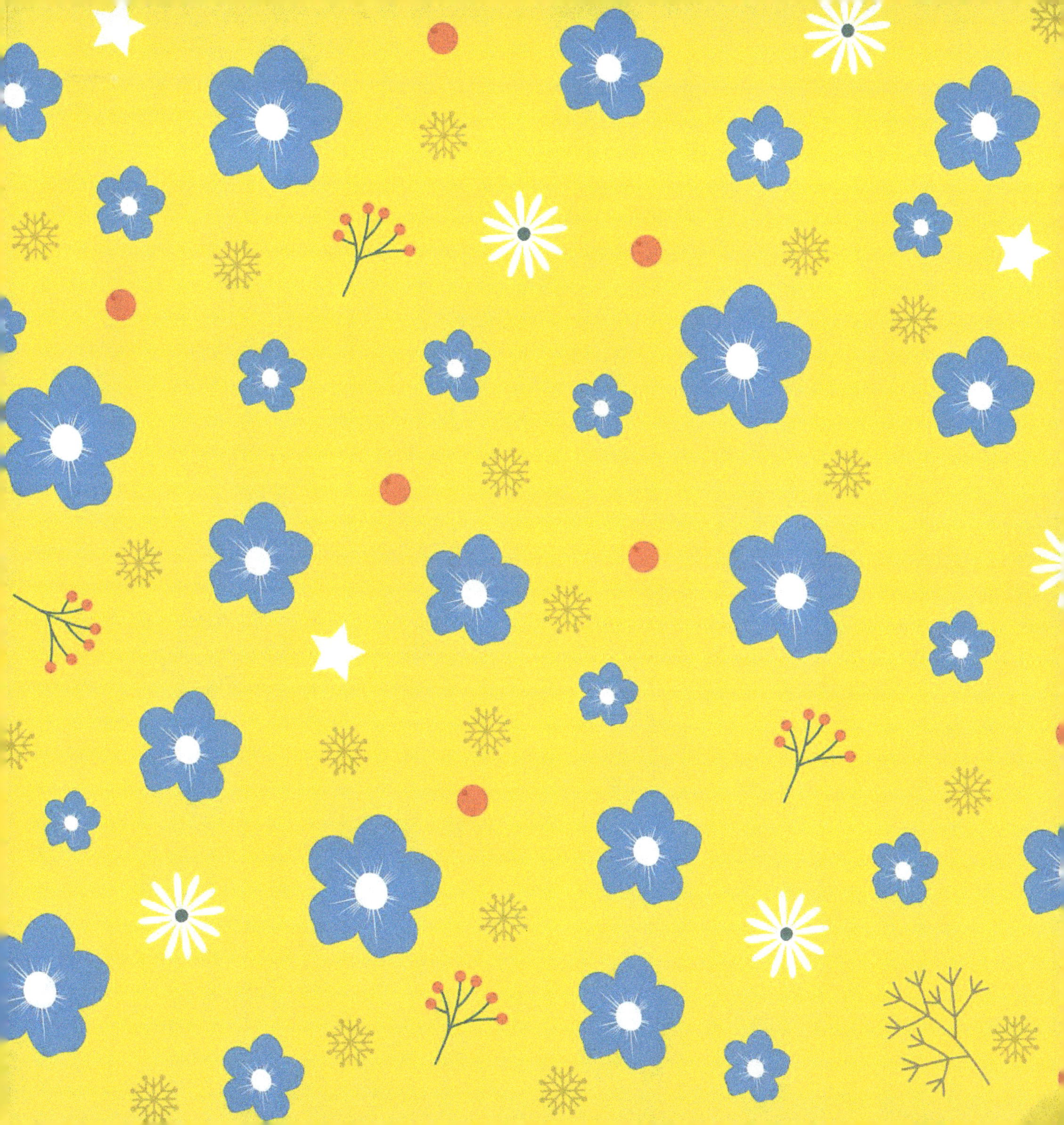

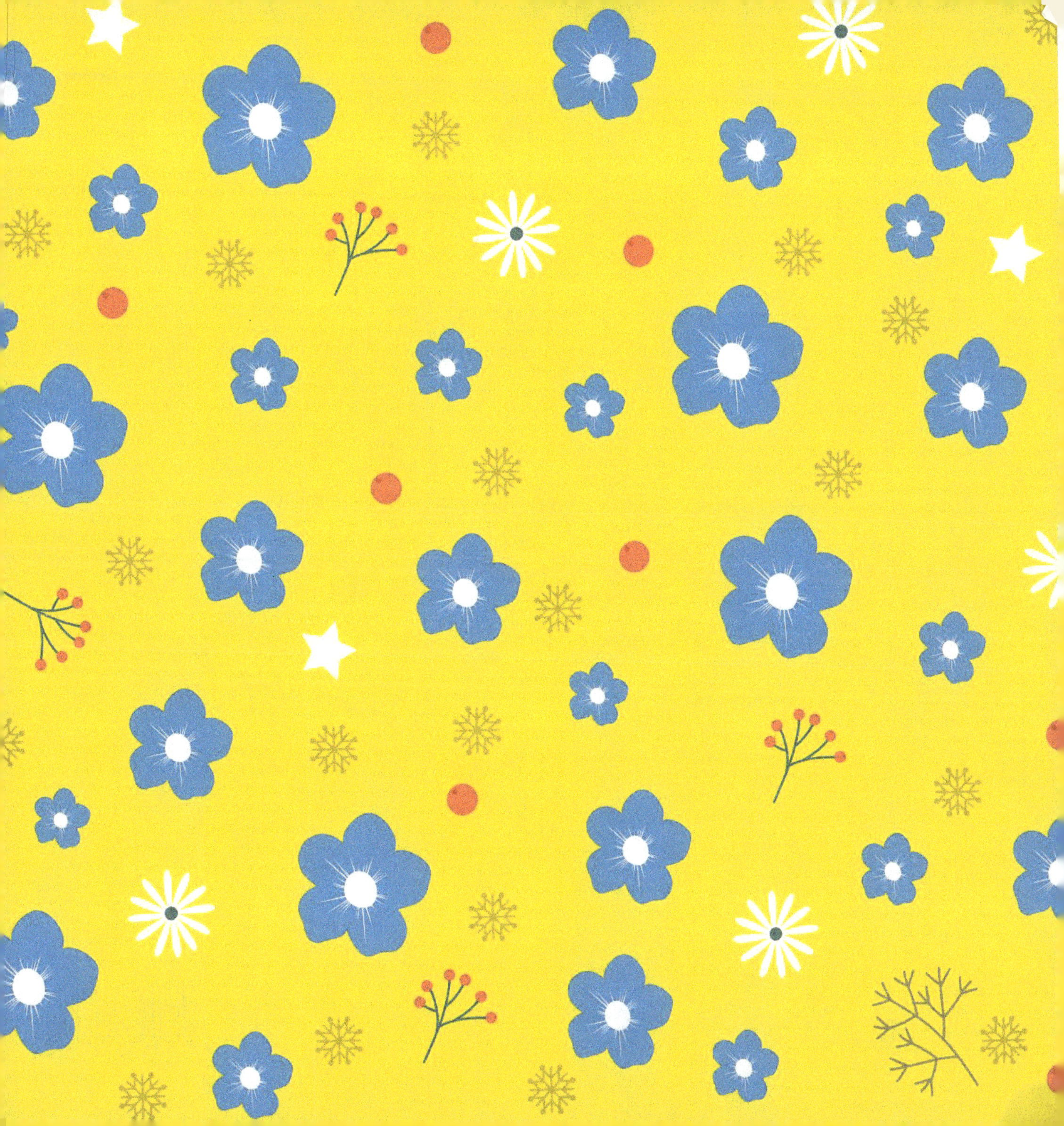

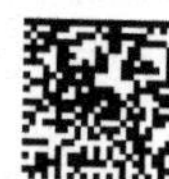

CPSIA information can be obtained
at www.ICGtesting.com
Printed in the USA
LVHW061733170522
718963LV00002B/9

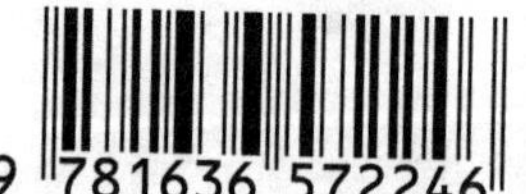

9 781636 572246